The Principles of Tajweed

The Children's Gift

تحفة الأطفال

Tuhfatul Adfaal

English - Arabic

Sh. Abdirahman Mohamed

Contents
المحتويات

Introduction
المقدمة

Tuhfatul Adfaal is a poem by Imam Al-Jamzury for those who wish to learn tajweed (Rules of Quranic recitation). It's shorter and easier than many other books.

يَقُـــولُ رَاجِـي رَحمـةِ الْغَفُـــورِ   دَوْمَـاً سُلَـــيْمَانُ هُـوَ الْجَمْـــزُورِى

Says he who steady longs for the mercy of the All-forgiving Benefactor,
Sulayman (bin Hussein bin Muhammad Affendi), who is from Jamzur.

الْحَمْـــدُ لِلَّـــهِ مُصَلِّـياً عَلــى   مُحَمَّـــدٍ وآلِـــهِ وَمَـنْ تَـلاَ

Praise be to Allah for allowing me to send prayers and reverence,
Upon Muhammad, his kin and those who followed him in deference.

وَبَعْـدُ هـذَا النَّـظْـمُ لِلْمُرِيـدِ   فــي النُّــونِ والتَّــنْوِينِ وَالْمُـدُودِ

Following that, this poem is for those who yearn to know,
the Nun Sakin, Tanween and Madd rules as they go.

سَــمَّيتُـــهُ بِتُحفَـــة الأَطْفَـالِ   عَـنْ شَيْـخِنَا الْمِيهِّي ذِي الْكَمـالِ

I have decided to title it "the Children's Gift,"
and relate from my sheikh Al-¬Meehiyi these precepts most perfect .

أَرْجُـــو بِــهِ أَنْ يَنْـفَعَ الطُّـلاَّبَـا   والأَجْـــرَ وَالْقَبُـــولَ وَالثَّوَابـا

I cherish that this proves of worth to its students,
and brings with it reward, reception and recompense.

Chapter one

The Rules of Nuun Saakin and Tanween
أحكام النون الساكنة والتنوين

Types of Nuuns & Tanween

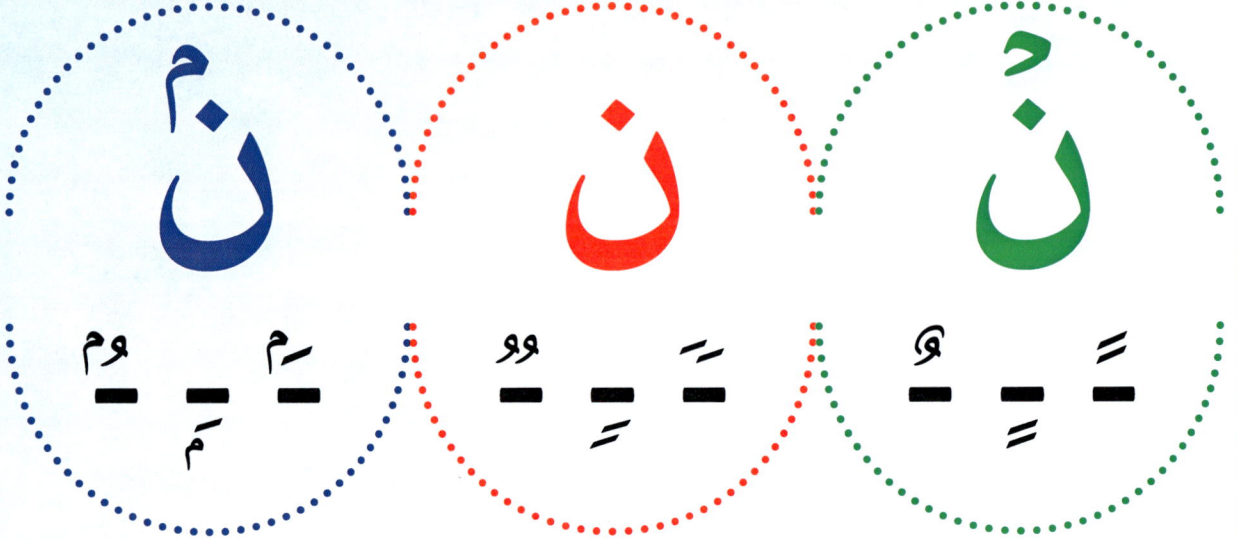

نٌ   نْ   نُّمْ

لِلنُّـــونِ إِنْ تَسْـــكُنْ وَلِلتَّـنْوِينِ أَرْبَـعُ أَحْكَـامٍ فَخُـذْ تَبْيِينِي

For the nun without vowels and the tanween diction,

exist four basic rules, so take my depiction.

Clear (Al-Idhhaar) الإظهار			Merging (Al-Idghaam) الإدغام		
ه	أ		ر	ي	
ح	ع		ل	م	
خ	غ		ن	و	

Turning (Al-Iqlaab) الإقلاب	ب

Concealment (Al-Ikhfaa') الإخفاء	ش	ج	ك	ق	ض	ط
	ص	ف	ت	د	ز	س
	ث	ذ	ظ			

فَـالأَوَّلُ الإِظْـهَـارُ قَبْـلَ أَحْـرُفِ   لِلْحَـلْـقِ سِـتٍّ رُتِّبَـتْ فَلْتَـعْـرِفِ

The first of these, the rule of Idhhaar, is before the letters hence, arising from the throat, six in number, in this known sequence:

In the rule of Al-idhhaar

- The Nuun will have visible sukuun
- The Dhammah tanween will be a 69 shape.
- The Fatha Tanween & Kasrah tanween will have equal parallel lines.
- The rule of Al-Idhhaar occurs if the following throat letters follows the Nuun with Sukuun:

هَمْـزٌ فَـهَـاءُ ثُـمَّ عَيْـنٌ حَـاءُ   مُهْمَلَـتَانِ ثُمَّ غَيْـنٌ خَـاءُ

Hamza and Hah, then Ain and Haa,
without the marks, then Ghain and Khaa.

There is in the throat three points for six letters, these three areas are:

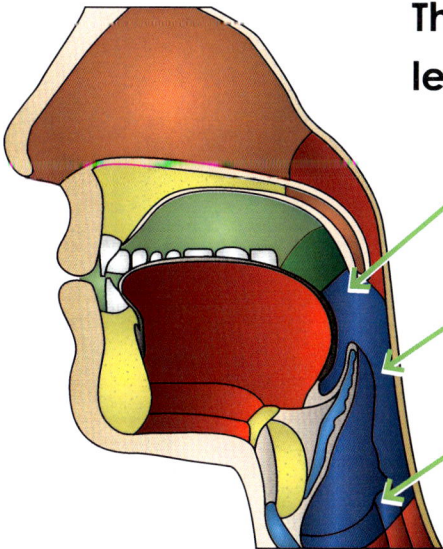

غ - خ	Top of the Throat	أدنى الحلق
ع - ح	Middle of the Throat	وسط الحلق
ء – ه	Bottom of the Throat	أقصى الحلق

Examples

النون الساكنة Nuun Saakin

﴿مَنْ أَنْبَأَكَ﴾ التحريم ٣	﴿وَيَنْئَوْنَ﴾ الأنعام ٢٦ (ولا ثاني لها)	ء
﴿مِنْ هَمَزَاتِ﴾ المؤمنون ٩٧	﴿تَنْهَرْ﴾ الضحى ١٠ ﴿مُنْهَمِرٍ﴾ القمر ١١	ه
﴿مِنْ عَلَقٍ﴾ العلق ٢	﴿أَنْعَمْتَ﴾ الفاتحة ﴿يَنْعِقُ﴾ البقرة ١٧١	ع
﴿لِمَنْ حَارَبَ﴾ التوبة ١٠٧	﴿يَنْحِتُونَ﴾ الحجر ٨٢ ﴿وَانْحَرْ﴾ الكوثر ٣	ح
﴿وَمَا مِنْ غَائِبَةٍ﴾ النمل ٧٥	﴿فَسَيُنْغِضُونَ﴾ الإسراء ٥١ (ولا ثاني لها)	غ
﴿وَلِمَنْ خَافَ﴾ الرحمن ٤٦	﴿وَالْمُنْخَنِقَةُ﴾ المائدة ٣	خ

التنوين Tanween

﴿كِتَابٌ أَنْزَلْنَهُ﴾	﴿حَاسِدٍ إِذَا﴾	﴿أَحَدًا أَبَدًا﴾	ء
﴿سَلَامٌ هِيَ﴾	﴿جُرُفٍ هَارٍ﴾	﴿وَنُوحًا هَدَيْنَا﴾	ه
﴿سَمِيعٌ عَلِيمٌ﴾	﴿وَلَيَالٍ عَشْرٍ﴾	﴿شَاكِرًا عَلِيمًا﴾	ع
﴿غَفُورٌ حَلِيمٌ﴾	﴿أَوَّابٍ حَفِيظٍ﴾	﴿نَارًا حَامِيَةً﴾	ح
﴿أَمْوَاتٌ غَيْرُ﴾	﴿مُحْصَنَاتٍ غَيْرَ﴾	﴿قَوْلًا غَيْرَ﴾	غ
﴿لَطِيفٌ خَبِيرٌ﴾	﴿سُنْبُلَتٍ خُضْرٍ﴾	﴿ثِيَابًا خُضْرًا﴾	خ

Merging
الإدغام

2

والثَّانِي إِدْغَامٌ بِسِتَّةٍ أَتَتْ   فِـي يَـرْمَـلُــونَ عِنْدَهُمْ قَـدْ ثَبَتَتْ

The second is Idgham, with six it takes effect,

in yarmaluun, a mnemonic which they accept.

In the Rule of Al-Idgaaam

- The Nuun has invisble Sukuun.
- The Tanween Dhammah has the look of number 99.
- The Tanween Fatha and Kasrah has unequal parallel lines.
- The Rule of Al-Idgaaam occurs If the following letters follow Nuun with Sukuun or Tanween:

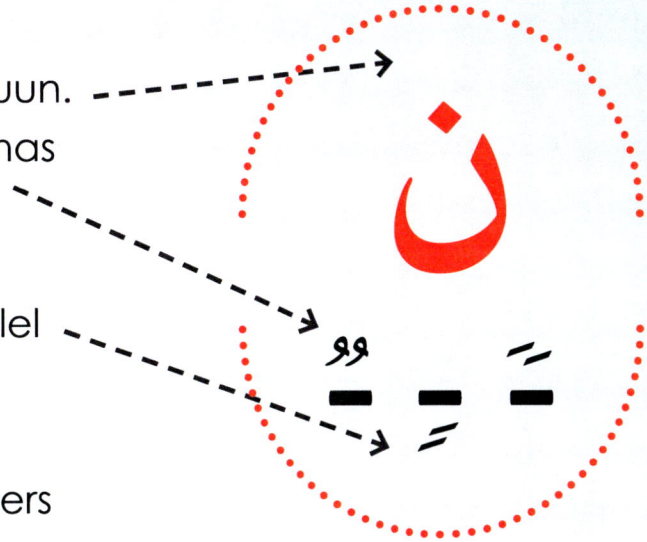

Its letters are:

لَـكِـنَّـهَا قِسْـمَـانِ قِسْـمٌ يُدْغَـمَـا   فِـيـهِ بِـغُـنَّـةٍ بِـيَـنْـمُو عُـلِـمَـا

But this is of two types, with the first being verbalized,

with the trait of ghunna, and by yanmu recognized.

7

إِلاَّ إِذَا كَانَا بِكِلْمَةٍ فَـلاَ   تُدْغِـمْ كَدُنْـيَا ثُـمَّ صِنْوَانٍ تَـلاَ

Except if this occurs within one word, then there is none,
no idgham in articulation, as in the words dunya and sinwan.

Idgaam means merging between two separate individual words. Therefore, it will not work on a single word,

For example: صِـنْوَانٍ

In this example, we have a Nuun with sukuun follow by a <u>Waaw</u> which include the letters of idgaam, but you cannot merge it and create ghunnah because Waaw is part of the same word.

Example 2: دُنْـيَا

Also in the <u>Dunyaa</u>, the Nuun saaakinah is followed a <u>Ya</u> which is amongst the letters of idgaam, however, no merging is required due to being a single word.

وَالثَّـانِـي إِدْغَـامٌ بِغَيْـرِ غُـنَّةْ   فِـي الـلاَّمِ وَالـرَّا ثُـمَّ كَرِّرَنَّـهْ

The second type is Idgham without the ghunna trait,
in lam and raa, but the latter you must reverberate.

ل	﴿لَئِن لَّمْ﴾	﴿ذِكْرٌ لِّلْعَٰلَمِينَ﴾
ر	﴿عَن رَّبِّهِم﴾	﴿لَرَءُوفٌ رَّحِيمٌ﴾

The sound of the Nuun and Tanween are totally silenced by the following Laam & Raa letters

Examples

النون الساكنة Nuun Saakin

		ي
﴿أَمَّن يُجِيبُ﴾ النمل ٦٢	﴿فَمَن يَسْتَمِعِ ٱلْأَنَ﴾ الجن ٩	ي
﴿لَن نَّدْخُلَهَآ أَبَدًا﴾ المائدة ٢٤	﴿إِن نَّفَعَتِ ٱلذِّكْرَىٰ﴾ الأعلى ٩	ن
﴿مِّن مَّالِ ٱللَّهِ﴾ النور ٣٣	﴿مِن مَّحِيصٍ﴾ إبراهيم ٢١	م
﴿مِن وَاقٍ﴾ الرعد ٣٤	﴿مِن وَلِيٍّ﴾ البقرة ١٠٧	و

التنوين Tanween

			ي
﴿أُمَّةٌ يَهْدُونَ﴾	﴿لِّقَوْمٍ يَعْقِلُونَ﴾	﴿يَوْمًا يَجْعَلُ﴾	ي
﴿بَخِعٌ نَّفْسَكَ﴾	﴿يَوْمَئِذٍ نَّاعِمَةٌ﴾	﴿عَذَابًا نُّكْرًا﴾	ن
﴿نَصِيبٌ مِّمَّا﴾	﴿وَظِلٍّ مَّمْدُودٍ﴾	﴿كِتَابًا مُّؤَجَّلًا﴾	م
﴿وَزَرْعٌ وَنَخِيلٌ﴾	﴿وَوَالِدٍ وَمَا وَلَدَ﴾	﴿طَيِّبًا وَٱشْكُرُوا﴾	و

3 Iqlaab
الإقلاب

وَّالثَّالِثُ الإِقْلَابُ عِنْدَ الْبَاءِ   مِيمـاً بِغُنَّـةٍ مَعَ الإِخْفَـاءِ

The third rule is Iqlab which occurs with the letter baa,
which is converted to meem and pronounced with Ikhfaa.

Tanween and Nuun Saakinah

Followed by

ب

ن

ـٌم ـٍم ـًم

﴿ وَمِنْ بَعْدِ ﴾

Iqlaab means changing from Nuun sound to a
meem sound. This requires Ghunnah and Small
gap between top and bottoms lips,

ب	النون الساكنة Nuun Saakin	
	﴿يَسْتَنۢبِطُونَهُۥ﴾	﴿أَنۢبِيَآءَ﴾ ﴿مِنۢ بَنِىٓ﴾ ﴿وَلَٰكِنۢ بَعُدَتۡ﴾
	﴿فَٱنۢبَجَسَتۡ﴾	﴿فَٱنۢبِذۡ﴾ ﴿لَئِنۢ بَسَطتَ﴾ ﴿مِّنۢ بَيۡنِنَآ﴾
	﴿ٱنۢبَعَاثَهُمۡ﴾	﴿أَنۢبَتَتۡ﴾ ﴿عَن بَيِّنَةٍ﴾ ﴿مِنۢ بَيۡتِكَ﴾

ب	التنوين Tanween		
	﴿نَفۡسًا بِغَيۡرِ﴾	﴿زَوۡجٍ بَهِيجٍ﴾	﴿مُؤَذِّنٌ بَيۡنَهُمۡ﴾
	﴿أَمَدًۢا بَعِيدًا﴾	﴿مَّشَّآءِۭ بِنَمِيمٍ﴾	﴿سَمِيعٌۢ بَصِيرٌ﴾

Ikhfaa
الإخفاء

وَالرَّابِعُ الإِخْفَاءُ عِنْدَ الْفَاضِلِ   مِنَ الْحُرُوفِ وَاجِبٌ لِلْفَاضِلِ

The fourth is Ikhfaa for the respected student,
with specified letters mandatory for the student.

In the Rule of Ikhfaa

- The Nuun has invisble Sukuun.
- The Tanween Dhammah has the look of number 99.
- The Tanween Fatha and Kasrah has unequal parallel lines.
- The Rule Ikhfaa occurs If the following letters follow Nuun with Sukuun or Tanween:

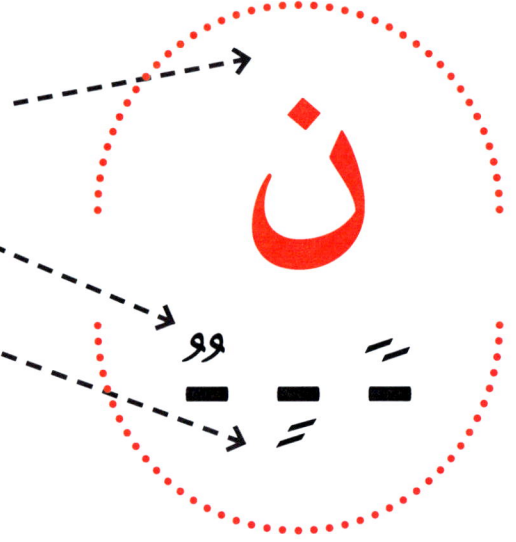

ن

ش	س	ز	ذ	د	ج	ث	ت
ك	ق	ف	ظ	ط	ض	ص	

﴿أَنذَرْنَـٰكُمْ﴾   ﴿فَمَن شَآءَ﴾

﴿يَوْمَئِذٍ شَأْنٌ﴾   ﴿وَكَأْسًا دِهَاقًا﴾

في خَمْسَةٍ مِنْ بَعْدِ عَشْرٍ رَمْزُهَا   فِي كِلْمِ هَذَا البَيْتِ قَدْ ضَمَّنْتُهَا

In fifteen letters it takes effect,
  within this prose that I erect:

صِفْ ذَا ثَنَا كَمْ جَادَ شَخْصٌ قَدْ سَمَا   دُمْ طَيِّبَاً زِدْ فِي تُقَىً ضَعْ ظَالِمَا

Relate of the praiseworthy one,
how excellent is he who achieves status robust;
  Be ever perpetual in virtue, cultivate piety,
    and fend off the one who is unjust.

Examples

ص	﴿مَنصُورًا﴾	﴿مِّن صِيَامٍ﴾	﴿عَمَلًا صَلِحًا﴾
ذ	﴿تُنذِرُهُم﴾	﴿وَمِن ذُرِّيَّتِي﴾	﴿ظِلٍّ ذِى ثَلَثٍ﴾
ث	﴿الْحِنثِ﴾	﴿مِن ثَمَرَةٍ﴾	﴿يَوْمَئِذٍ ثَمَنِيَةٌ﴾
ك	﴿أَنكَالًا﴾	﴿لَئِن كَشَفْتَ﴾	﴿مَلَكٌ كَرِيمٌ﴾
ج	﴿فَأَنجَهُ﴾	﴿وَإِن جَنَحُواْ﴾	﴿خَلْقًا جَدِيدًا﴾
ش	﴿نُنشِرُهَا﴾	﴿مِن شَعَآئِرِ﴾	﴿رَسُولًا شَهِدًا﴾
ق	﴿يَنقَلِبْ﴾	﴿مِن قَرِيبٍ﴾	﴿رِزْقًا قَالُواْ﴾

Examples

﴿بَشَرًا سَوِيًّا﴾	﴿مَن سَفِهَ﴾	﴿فَأَنسَلهُ﴾	س
﴿وَكَأْسًا دِهَاقًا﴾	﴿مِن دِيَرِهِمْ﴾	﴿سُندُسٍ﴾	د
﴿قَوْمًا طَٰغِينَ﴾	﴿أَن طَهِّرَا﴾	﴿ٱلْمُقَنطَرَةِ﴾	ط
﴿غُلَٰمًا زَكِيًّا﴾	﴿فَإِن زَلَلْتُم﴾	﴿أَنزَلَ﴾	ز
﴿يَتِيمًا فَـَٔاوَىٰ﴾	﴿فَمَن فَرَضَ﴾	﴿أَنفَقْتُم﴾	ف
﴿صَٰلِحًا تَرْضَهُ﴾	﴿وَلَن تَفْعَلُواْ﴾	﴿ءَامَنتُ﴾	ت
﴿مَكَانًا ضَيِّقًا﴾	﴿عَن ضَلَٰلَتِهِم﴾	﴿مَّنضُودٍ﴾	ض
﴿ظِلًّا ظَلِيلًا﴾	﴿وَلَٰكِن ظَلَمُوٓاْ﴾	﴿تَنظُرُونَ﴾	ظ

Meem with Shaddah
الميم المشددة

﴿فَأَمَّا﴾

﴿فَأُمُّهُ﴾

﴿ٱلْيَمِّ﴾

Nuun with Shaddah
النون المشددة

﴿ٱلنَّاسِ﴾

﴿ٱلْخَنَّاسِ﴾

﴿ٱلظَّنِّ﴾

وَغُــنَّ مِيــماً ثُــمَّ نُونًـا شُــدِّدَا   وَسَـــمِّ كُــلاً حَــرْفَ غُنَّــةٍ بَــدَا

And articulate ghunnah of the nun and meem
that carries the double accent,

and refer to both as letters of ghunna,
as is obvious and apparent.

Examples

﴿بِجَهَنَّمَ﴾ ﴿بِٱلنَّاصِيَةِ﴾ ﴿ٱلنَّاسِ﴾ ﴿لَتَرَوُنَّ﴾ ﴿أَنَّ﴾

﴿إِنَّآ﴾ ﴿فَأُمُّهُ﴾ ﴿فَأَمَّا﴾ ﴿وَأَمَّا﴾ ﴿عَمَّ﴾

			الميم
﴿فَأُمُّهُ﴾	﴿ٱلْمُزَّمِّلُ﴾	﴿مُحَمَّدٌ﴾ ﴿حَمَّالَةَ﴾	
﴿لَيُسَمُّونَ﴾	﴿سَمَّاعُونَ﴾	﴿ثُمَّ﴾ ﴿لَمَّا﴾	
﴿ٱلنُّورِ﴾	﴿ٱلنِّسَآءَ﴾	﴿جَنَّـٰتِ ٱلنَّعِيمِ﴾	النون
﴿يَظُنُّونَ﴾	﴿وَيُمَنِّيهِمْ﴾	﴿إِنَّ﴾ ﴿كَأَنَّ﴾	

Chapter Two

The Rules of Meem with Sukuun
أحكام الميم الساكنة

وَالمِيـمُ إِنْ تَسْـكُنْ تَـجِى قَبْلَ الْهِجَا   لاَ أَلِـفٍ لَيِّـنَةٍ لِـذِى الْحِـجَا

When stopping on Meem before the letters of the alphabet,
but not before the Alif Layyinah, for he who is intelligent,

Types of Meem with Sukuun

Meem with **visible** sukuun   مْ   مْ   Meem with **invisible** sukuun

Meem with Sukuun has three rules and is read three different
way according to the letter following by the meem with sukuun.

أَحْكَامُـهَا ثَلاَثَـةٌ لِمَـنْ ضَبَـطْ   إِخْفَاءُ ادْغَامٌ وَإِظْهَـارٌ فَقَـطْ

are three rules for he who would save them to memory,
and they are the rules of Ikhfaa, Idgham and Idhhar only.

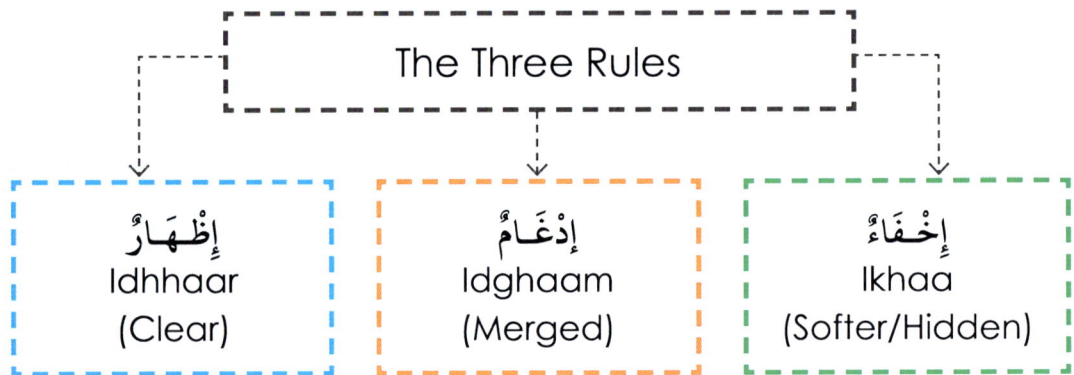

The Three Rules

| إِظْهَارٌ Idhhaar (Clear) | إِدْغَامٌ Idghaam (Merged) | إِخْفَاءُ Ikhaa (Softer/Hidden) |

فَالأَوَّلُ الإِخْفَاءُ عِنْدَ الْبَاءِ   وَسَمِّهِ الشَّفَوِيَّ لِلْقُرَّاءِ

The first is Ikhfa with the baa letter,
named Lips Ikhfaa by the recitors.

م < ب

Meem with sukuun
Followed by

Meem & Ba
Are pronounced
from the lips

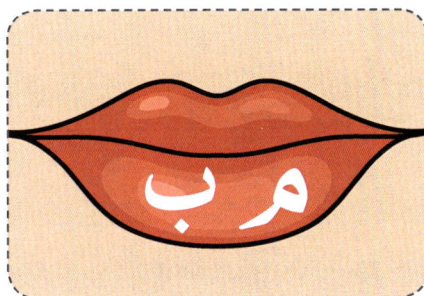

م ب

Softer meem transit into the Ba with Ghunnah

Examples

﴿وَكَلْبُهُم بَٰسِطٞ﴾	﴿إِنَّ رَبَّهُم بِهِمۡ﴾
﴿وَمَا هُم بِمُؤۡمِنِينَ﴾	﴿وَلَسۡتُم بِـَٔاخِذِيهِ﴾
﴿يَعۡتَصِم بِٱللَّهِ﴾	﴿تَرۡمِيهِم بِحِجَارَةٖ﴾
﴿إِن كُنتُم بِـَٔايَٰتِهِۦ مُؤۡمِنِينَ﴾	﴿وَأَنِ ٱحۡكُم بَيۡنَهُم﴾

الْبَاء (ب)

2 Idghaam (Merging)
إِدْغَامٌ

وَسَـمِّ إِدْغَامًا صَغِـيرًا يَـا فَـتَـى   وَالثَّانِـى إِدْغَـامٌ بِمِثْـلِـهَـا أَتَـى

The second is Idghaam when its likeness (of a meem) appears
and name it the Lesser Idghaam young man.

مّ > م

Meem with sukuun
Followed by

Merged together
with second meem

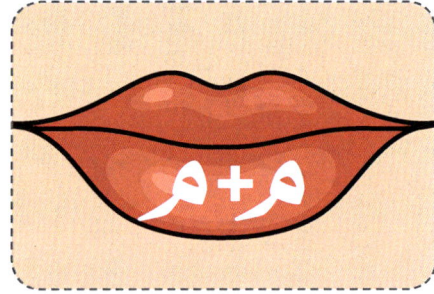

م + مّ

Examples

﴿إِن كُنتُم مُّؤْمِنِينَ﴾	﴿فِى قُلُوبِهِم مَّرَضٌ﴾
﴿جَزَآؤُهُم مَّغْفِرَةٌ﴾	﴿وَلَقَدْ جَآءَكُم مُّوسَىٰ﴾
﴿وَأَنتُم مُّسْلِمُونَ﴾	﴿فَإِذَآ أَفَضْتُم مِّنْ عَرَفَٰتٍ﴾
﴿أَطْعَمَهُم مِّن جُوعٍ﴾	﴿وَلَهُم مَّا يَشْتَهُونَ﴾
﴿يَنصُرُكُم مِّن دُونِ﴾	﴿وَءَامَنَهُم مِّنْ خَوْفٍ﴾
﴿وَٱللَّهُ يَعِدُكُم مَّغْفِرَةً﴾	﴿مِنكُم مَّن يُرِيدُ ٱلدُّنْيَا﴾

وَالثَّالِـثُ الإِظْهَـارُ فِى الْبَقِيَّـةِ — مِـنْ أَحْـرُفٍ وَسَمِّـهَا شَفْوِيَّـهْ

The third is Idhhaar which occurs with the balance of the letters,
and Named Lipped Idhhaar in our expression

In Idhhaar, the Sukuun will be **(Visible)**
Unlike the other rules

مْ

Meem with sukuun
Followed by

> 26
Letters

وَاحْـذَرْ لَدَى وَاوٍ وَفَـا أَنْ تَخْتَـفِي — لِقُـرْبِـهَا وَلاتحـادِ فَاعْـرِفِ

And be wary of making Ikhfa with waw and faa when you read,
due to the closeness and unity of its makhraj, so take heed.

The letters share the same position (Makhraj) of
pronunciation; however, they differ upon ruling here.

⚠️ Be wary of making Ikhfaa when meem is followed by (و,ف) Because is Al-Idhhaar

ب م ف و

The rule of Idghaam and The rule of Ikhfaa (ب,م) Applies on thses two letters

19

Examples

﴿سَنُدْخِلُهُمْ جَنَّتٍ﴾

﴿وَظَنَنتُمْ ظَنَّ ٱلسَّوْءِ﴾

﴿جَعَلَكُمْ خُلَفَآءَ﴾

﴿رَمْزًا﴾

﴿فَهُمْ غَٰفِلُونَ﴾

﴿أَمْ أَنتُمْ صَٰمِتُونَ﴾

﴿وَقَوْلِهِمْ قُلُوبُنَا﴾

﴿سَوَآءٌ عَلَيْهِمْ ءَأَنذَرْتَهُمْ أَمْ لَمْ تُنذِرْهُمْ﴾

﴿تَمْسَسْكُمْ﴾

﴿يَمْحُواْ﴾

﴿لَعَلَّهُمْ يَتَّقُونَ﴾

﴿وَإِذْ قَتَلْتُمْ نَفْسًا﴾

﴿جَآءَكُمْ ذِكْرٌ﴾

﴿وَأَمْدَدْنَٰكُم﴾

﴿فِى قُلُوبِهِمْ زَيْغٌ﴾

﴿أَلَمْ أَقُل لَّكُمْ﴾

﴿حَيْثُ شِئْتُمْ رَغَدًا﴾

﴿بِحَمْدِ﴾

Chapter Three

The Rules of Laam with Sukuun in Nouns and Verbs
أحكام اللام الساكنة في الأسماء والأفعال

أُولَاهُمَا إِظْهَارُهَا فَلْتَعْرِفِ   لِلَّامِ أَلْ حَالَانِ قَبْلَ الْأَحْرُفِ

The lam of the definite article exists in two states before the letters,
the first is its manifest articulation, and should be understood better

Types of Laam

Sun Letters
14

Moon Letters
14

مِنَ ابْغِ حَجَّكَ وَخَفْ عَقِيمَهُ   قَبْلَ أرْبَعٍ مَعَ عَشَرَةٍ خُذْ عِلْمَهُ

Occurring before fourteen letters, so learn them well,
from this mnemonic: "Seek your goal and futile pursuits repel."

The moon letters if they come after (ال)
The laam takes sukuun and is pronounced
clearly (AL).

﴿أَهْلِ ٱلْكِتَبِ﴾

Examples

﴿ٱلْخَبِيرُ﴾	خ	﴿هُوَ ٱلْأَوَّلُ وَٱلْآخِرُ﴾	ا
﴿ٱلْفَتَّاحُ﴾	ف	﴿ٱلْبَارِئُ﴾	ب
﴿ٱلْعَزِيزُ ٱلْعَلِيمُ﴾	ع	﴿وَرَبُّكَ ٱلْغَنِيُّ﴾	غ
﴿ٱلْقَادِرُ﴾	ق	﴿ٱلْحَمِيدُ﴾	ح
﴿ٱلْيَمِينِ﴾	ي	﴿ٱلْجَبَّارُ﴾	ج
﴿ٱلْمُؤْمِنُ﴾	م	﴿ٱلْكَرِيمُ﴾	ك
﴿ٱلْهُدَى﴾	ه	﴿ٱلْوَكِيلُ﴾	و

21

ثَانِيهِـــمَا إِدْغَامُـــهَا فِى أَرْبَــعٍ وَعَشْـرَةٍ أَيْـضاً وَرَمْـزَهَا فَـعِ

The second is its assimilation, which in fourteen does exist,
and likewise, facilitate your recollection of them from this:

طِبْ ثُمَّ صِـلْ رُحْمَاً تَفُـزْ ضِـفْ ذَا نِعَم دَعْ سُـوءَ ظَنٍ زُرْ شَرِيـفاً لِلْكَـرَم

Be meritorious, maintain relations for success,
and host those who are beneficent;

Shun ill estimations of others,
and frequent the noble one for munificence.

﴿عَنِ ٱلنَّعِيمِ﴾ = ﴿عَنِنْ نَعِيمٍ﴾

← - - - - The Sun letters if they come after (ال), The letter after laam takes Shaddah and the Laam is silenced

Examples

﴿ٱلنَّعِيمِ﴾	ن	﴿ٱلطَّيِّبَٰتُ﴾	ط
﴿ٱلدُّعَآءَ﴾	د	﴿ٱلثَّوَابَ﴾	ث
﴿ٱلسَّكِينَةَ﴾	س	﴿ٱلصَّٰبِرِينَ﴾	ص
﴿ٱلظَّهِيرَةِ﴾	ظ	﴿ٱلرَّحْمَٰنِ ٱلرَّحِيمِ﴾	ر
﴿ٱلزَّٰهِدِينَ﴾	ز	﴿ٱلتَّٰٓئِبُونَ﴾	ت
﴿ٱلشَّٰهِدِينَ﴾	ش	﴿ٱلضُّعَفَٰٓؤُاْ﴾	ض
﴿ٱللَّطِيفُ﴾	ل	﴿ٱلذِّكْرَىٰ﴾	ذ

وَاللاَّمَ الأُولَـى سَمِّـهَا قَمْـرِيَّـهْ   وَاللاَّمَ الأُخْـرَى سَمِّـهَا شَمْسِـيَّهْ

Name the first Lam Qamariya, (Moon letters)
and the latter Lam Shamsiyyah (Sun letters).

وَأَظْهِـرَنَّ لاَمَ فِعْـلٍ مُطْلَـقاً   فِى نَحْـوِ قُلْ نَعَمْ وَقُلْنَـا وَالْتَقَى

And pronounce with manifestation the verbal lam consistently,
in words like Qul Naam, Qulna, Waltaqaa and their variety.

Laam in verbs is always
clearly pronounced

End	Middle	Beginning
❀ قُلْ ❀	❀ قُلْنَا ❀	❀ الْتَقَى ❀

End	Middle	Beginning	
ث	ت	ب	ا
د	خ	ح	ج
س	ز	ر	ذ
ط	ض	ص	ش
ف	غ	ع	ظ
م	ل	ك	ق
ي	هـ	و	ن

23

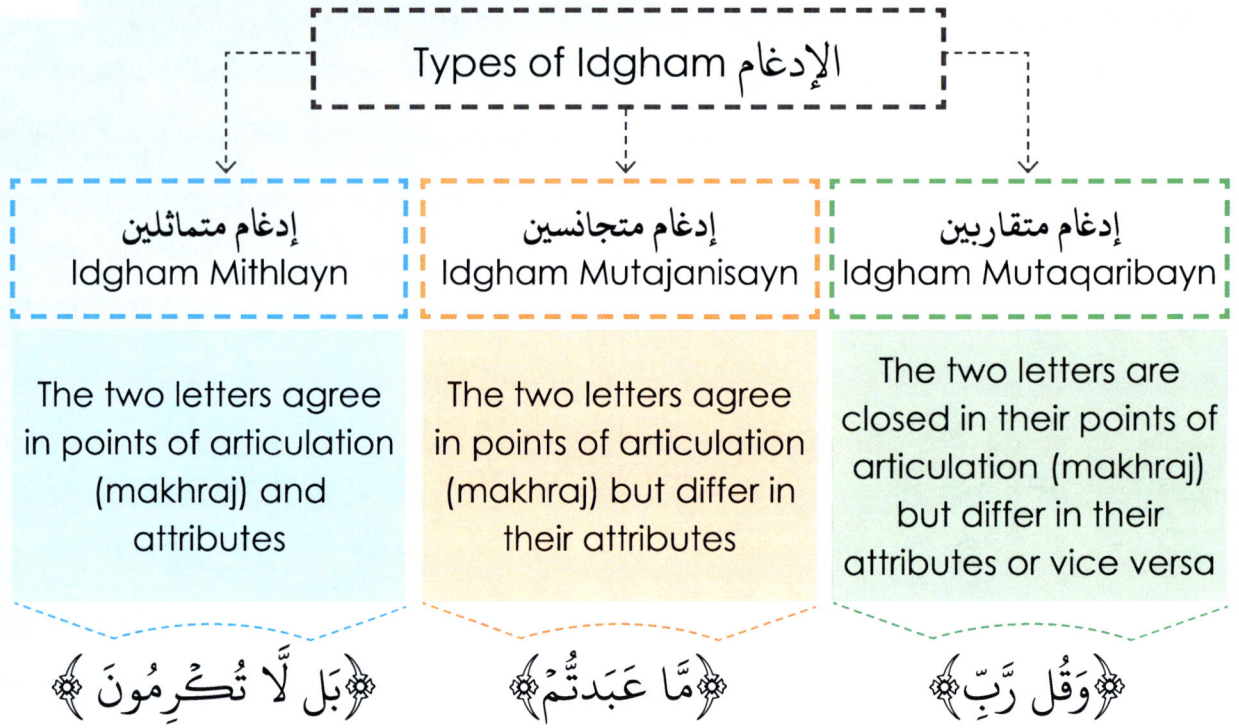

Types of Idgham [Mithlayn, Mutaqaribayn and Mutajanisayn]
المثلين والمتقاربين والمتجانسين

```
Types of Idgham الإدغام
```

إدغام متماثلين Idgham Mithlayn	إدغام متجانسين Idgham Mutajanisayn	إدغام متقاربين Idgham Mutaqaribayn
The two letters agree in points of articulation (makhraj) and attributes	The two letters agree in points of articulation (makhraj) but differ in their attributes	The two letters are closed in their points of articulation (makhraj) but differ in their attributes or vice versa
﴿بَل لَّا تُكۡرِمُونَ﴾	﴿مَّا عَبَدتُّمۡ﴾	﴿وَقُل رَّبِّ﴾

إِنْ فِي الصِّفَـاتِ وَالْمَخَـارِجِ اتَّفَـقْ   حَـرْفَانِ فَالْمِثْـلَانِ فِيهِـمَا أَحَـقْ

If two letters agree in attribute and point of articulation,
then it is more deserving to use the Mithlayn designation.

Definition of 5 major areas

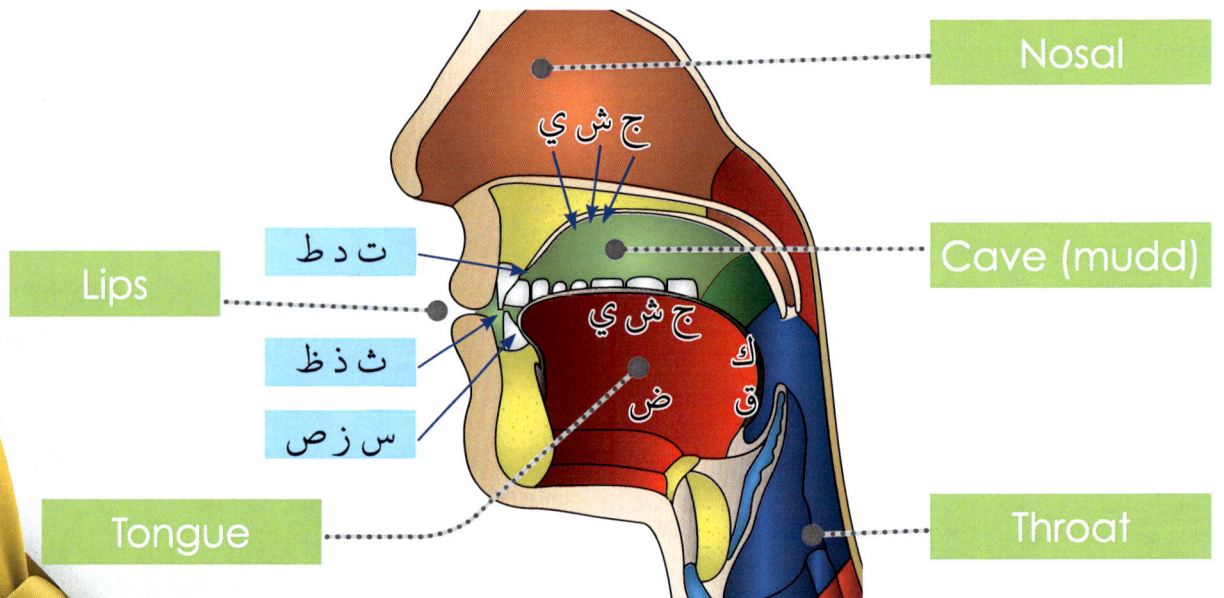

- Nosal
- Cave (mudd)
- Throat
- Lips
- Tongue

جـ شـ يـ

ت د ط
ث ذ ظ
س ز ص

جـ شـ يـ
كـ
ق ض

وَإِنْ يَكُونَا مَخْرَجاً تَقَارَبَا   وَفِي الصِّفَاتِ اخْتَلَفَا يُلَقَّبَا

But if the two in their points of articulation be akin,
          yet in their attributes varying then use the heading

مُتَقَارِبَيْنِ أَوْ يَكُونَا اتَّفَقَا   فِي مَخْرَجٍ دُونَ الصِّفَاتِ حُقِّقَا

Mutaqaribayn; And if they so happen to concur
          in articulation but not attribute then they deserve

بِالْمُتَجَانِسَيْنِ ثُمَّ إِنْ سَكَنْ   أَوَّلُ كُلٍّ فَالصَّغِيرَ سَمِّيَنْ

Mutajanisayn; And if its status be without vowel of
          the first letter in each case, the Lesser is the title

أَوْ حُرِّكَ الْحَرْفَانِ فِى كُلٍّ فَقُلْ   كُلٌّ كَبِيرُ وافْهَمَنْهُ بِالْمُثُلْ

And if both the letters are with vowels in all the situations,
          then term it the Greater, and learn this with illustrations

المتجانسان

هما الحرفان اللذان اتحدا مخرجاً واختلفا صفة.

أقسامه:

صغير
الحرف الأول ساكناً والثاني متحركاً.
حكمه: يجب إدغامه.
حروفه: [د، ت] [ت، د] [ت، ط] [ط، ت] [ذ، ظ] [ذ، ث] [ب، م]
﴿وَقَد تَّبَيَّنَ﴾، ﴿أَثْقَلَت دَّعَوَا﴾، ﴿أَحَطتُ﴾

كبير
أن يكون الحرفان متحركين.
حكمه: الإظهار.
﴿الصَّٰلِحَٰتِ طُوبَىٰ﴾

مطلق
الحرف الأول متحركاً والثاني ساكناً.
حكمه: الإظهار.
﴿مَّبْعُوثُونَ﴾، ﴿أَفَتَطْمَعُونَ﴾

Chapter Five

Madd (prolongation of Words)
أقسام المد

وَالمَـدُّ أَصْلِـىٌّ وَ فَـرْعِـىٌّ لَـهُ   وَسَـمِّ أَوَّلاً طَبِيعِـيّاً وَهُـو

Mad exists in two types, they being Natural and Derived,
so name the initial one Natural and it is comprised

فرعي Derived/Long madd	أصلي Natural / Short madd

ي	ا	و

HOW MADD IS MADE

There are three vowels in the Arabic Language:

Dhammah بُ BU	Kasrah بِ BE	Fathah بَ BA

- In order to make the Letter with Fathah (بَ) longer we add Alif (ا) and it becomes (بَا) BAA.

- In order to make the Letter with Kasrah (بِ) longer we add Ya (ي) and it becomes (بِي) BEE.

- In order to make the Letter with Dhammah (بُ) longer we add Waaw (و) and it becomes (بُو) BUU

مَـالاَ تَوَقُّـفُ لَـهُ عَـلَـى سَـبَـبْ ⟵ وَلاَبِـدُونِهِ الحُـرُوفُ تُجْتَـلَـبْ

Of that madd which on a cause does not rely,

And neither can its letters without it be realised.

بَـلْ أَيُّ حَـرْفٍ غَـيْـرُ هَـمْـزٍ أَوْ سُـكُـونْ ⟵ جَـا بَـعْـدَ مَـدٍّ فَالطَّبِـيِـعِيَّ يَكُـونْ

But if any letter, without hamza, or sukoon

follows the madd, then arises the Natural/Short brand madd.

THE FIRST TYPE OF MADD

The short, default madd is know as **MADDUL ASLEE or Madd Dabee'ee**. This madd is usually two vowels long. AA, EE, UU.

Example

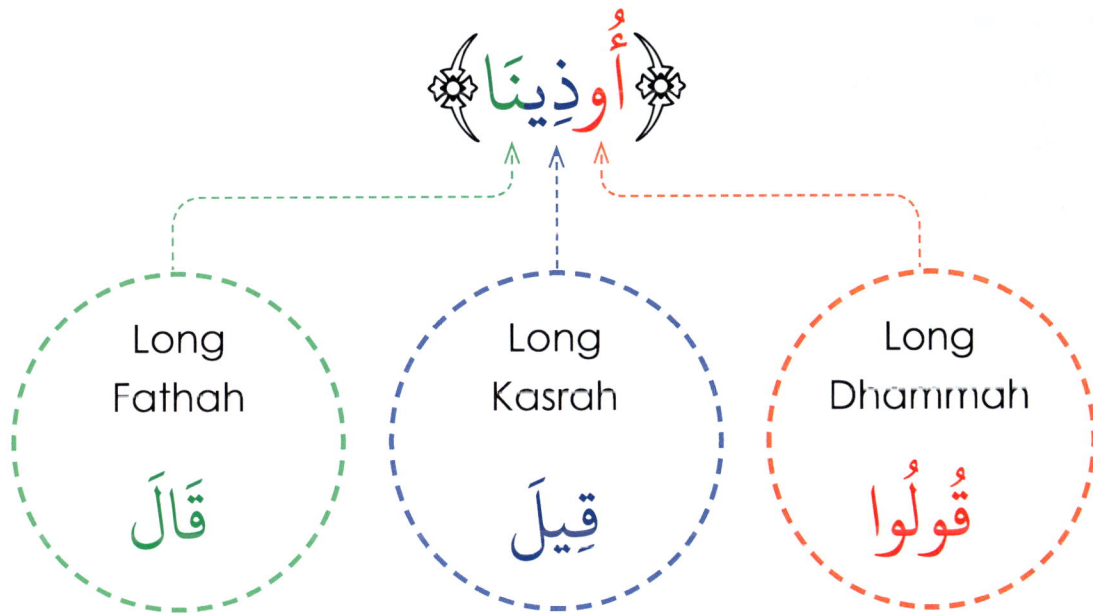

Long Fathah — قَالَ

Long Kasrah — قِيلَ

Long Dhammah — قُولُوا

THE SECOND TYPE OF MADD

وَالآخَـرُ الْفَرْعِـيُّ مَوْقُـوفٌ عَلـي   سَـبَبْ كَهَمْـزٍ أَوْ سُـكُونٍ مُسْـجَـلاً

The second type is the Derived madd which rests upon a cause,
namely, always on the hamza letter or sukoon.

If natural short (Maddul Aslee) is followed by:

Sukuun	Shaddah	Hamza
﴿ءَآلْـَٔنَ﴾	﴿ٱلْحَآقَّةُ﴾	﴿جَآءَ﴾

Then it becomes Maddul Far'ee

Maddul-Far'ee is derived from Maddul-Aslee.

حُرُوفُـهُ ثَـلاَثَـةٌ فَعِيـهَا   مِـنْ لَفْـظِ وَايٍ وَهْىَ فى نُوحِيـهَا

The madd has three letters, so know them as explained,
in the mnemonic wai and in the word nuuheehaa contained.

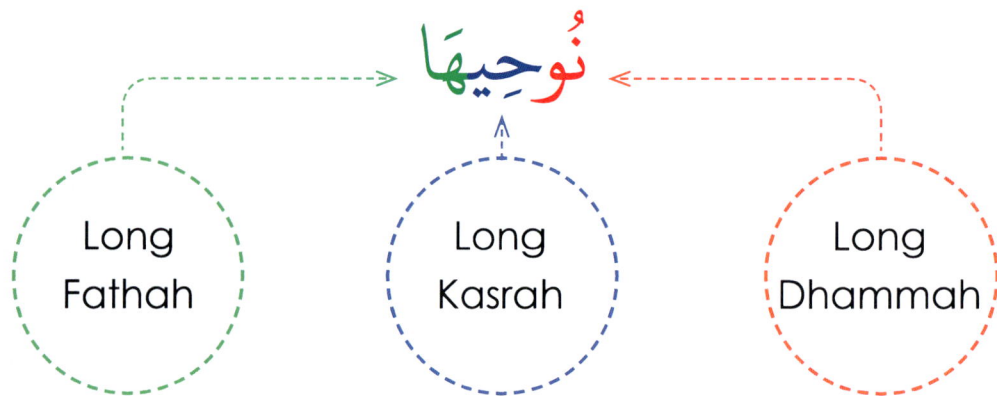

نُوحِيهَا

Long Fathah	Long Kasrah	Long Dhammah

وَالْكَسْرُ قَبْلَ الْيَا وَقَبْلَ الْوَاوِ ضَمّ   شَـرْطٌ وَفَـتْحٌ قَبْـلَ أَلِـفٍ يُلْـتَـزَمْ

And kasra before the letter ya,
and waw with dhamma preceding,

is surely a condition, whereas the fatha
before the alif is binding.

وَاللِّـيْنُ مِنْـهَا الْيَا وَوَاوٌ سَكَـنَا   إِنِ انْفِـتَـاحٌ قَبْـلَ كُـلٍّ أُعْـلِـنَا

And from these are the Layyin letters: waw and yaa sakin,
when preceded by the vowel fatha, as is plainly lucent.

A gentler Madd or Maddul-Leen is a Madd created when you stop in word containing Waw with Sukun or Ya with Sukuun proceeded by a letter with Fathah.

﴿خَوْفٍ﴾

Fathah followed
by Waw

﴿الْبَيْتِ﴾

Fathah followed
by Ya

This Madd only appears when we stop at the word

And is also prolonged between 2, 4 or 6 vowels

Chapter Six

The ruling of Madd/Elongation
أحكام المد

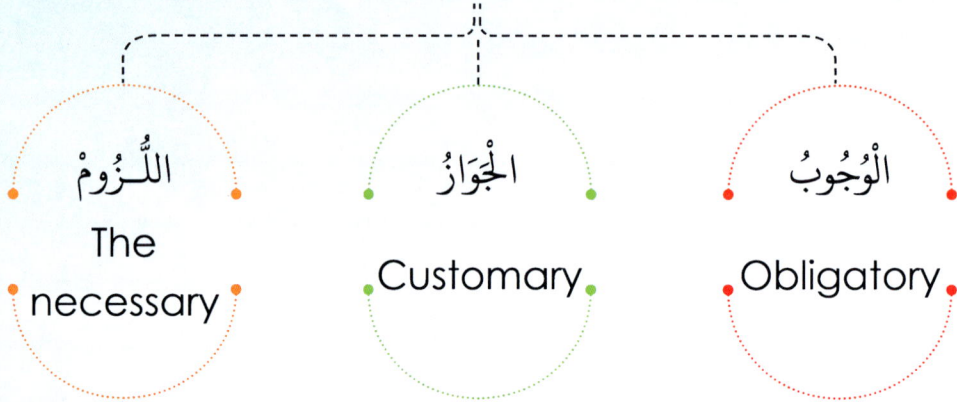

اللُّزُومْ	الْجْوَازْ	الْوُجُوبْ
The necessary	Customary	Obligatory

وَهِـــيَ الْوُجُـوبُ وَالْجَـوَازُ وَاللُّـزُومْ   لِلْمَــدِّ أَحْكَــامٌ ثَلَاثَــةٌ تَــدُومْ

The derived madd, its rules are always three;
and they are Wajib, Ja'iz and Lazim only.

Waajib (Obligatory)   4 beats long

فِـي كِلْمَـةٍ وَذَا بِمُتَّصِـلٍ يُعَـدْ   فَـوَاجِبٌ إِنْ جَـاءَ هَمْـزٌ بَعْـدَ مَـدْ

And Wajib is when hamza, after a letter of madd does follow,
in one single word, and this is termed Madd Muttasil also.

﴿ جَاۤءُوكَ ﴾   ﴿ أُوْلَـٰۤئِكَ ﴾

Jaaiz (Customary)   2 or 4 beats long

كُـلٌّ بِكِلْمَـةٍ وَهَـذَا الْمُنْفَصِـلْ   وَجَائِـزٌ مَـدٌّ وَقَصْـرٌ إِنْ فُصِـلْ

And Jaiz is when prolongation and shortening are acceptable,
when they are in separate words, and this is also termed Madd

﴿ وَمَاۤ أَدْرَىٰكَ ﴾   ﴿ إِنَّاۤ أَعْطَيْنَـٰكَ ﴾

Aaridh-lil sukun   2 , 4 or 6 beats long

وَمِثْـلُ ذَا إِنْ عَـرَضَ السُّكُـونُ   وَقْـفَاً كَتَعْـلَـمُـونَ نَسْتَعِـينُ

And likewise is the case where the sukoon is created,
from stopping, in the words ta'lamoon and nasta'een illustrated.

Madd For Stopping at the end of a Word is
called **Aaridh-Lil sukun**.

﴿ بِسْمِ ٱللَّهِ ٱلرَّحْمَٰنِ ٱلرَّحِيمِ ١ ﴾

ٱلْحَمْدُ لِلَّهِ رَبِّ ٱلْعَٰلَمِينَ ٢ ٱلرَّحْمَٰنِ ٱلرَّحِيمِ ٣ مَٰلِكِ يَوْمِ ٱلدِّينِ ٤

إِيَّاكَ نَعْبُدُ وَإِيَّاكَ نَسْتَعِينُ ٥ ٱهْدِنَا ٱلصِّرَٰطَ ٱلْمُسْتَقِيمَ ٦

صِرَٰطَ ٱلَّذِينَ أَنْعَمْتَ عَلَيْهِمْ غَيْرِ ٱلْمَغْضُوبِ عَلَيْهِمْ وَلَا ٱلضَّآلِّينَ ٧ ﴾

The elongation should consistent throughout 2, 4 or 6 beats long.

Madd-badal   2 , 4 or 6 beats long

أَوْ قُـدِّمَ الْهَمْـزُ عَلَـي الْمَـدِّ وَذَا   بَـدَلْ كَآمَـنُوا وَإِيمَاناً خُـذَا

But in those cases the hamza precedes the madd letter,
arises the Madd Badal, in aamanu and imaanaa illustrated.

- Al-Madd Al-Badal is a kind of Al-Madd Al-Tabee'ee.
- It occurs when a word has two following hamzas (ء) as the second hamza is converted to Alif, Waw, or Yaa depending on the Haraka of the first Hamza.
- The formed Alif, Waw, or Yaa will have Madd tabee'ee and is Sounded for two counts.

﴿إِيمَٰنًا﴾   ﴿أُوتُوا﴾   ﴿ءَامَنُوا﴾

Laazim (Compulsory) 6 beats long

وَلَازِمٌ إِنِ السُّكُونُ أُصِّـــلاَ   وَصْـلاً وَوَقْـفـأً بَعْـدَ مَـدٍّ طُـوِّلاَ

And Lazim occurs when real is the stop, after the madd,

in flow and stop, and in length there can be no drop.

- -

أَقْسَـــامُ لاَزِمٍ لَـدَيهِم أَرْبَعَــة   وَتِــلْكَ كِـلْمِـيٌّ وَحَرْفِـيٌّ مَعَـهْ

The types of Lazim among them2 are four,

and they are either the Kalimi or Harfi sort.

- -

كِلاَهُـمَا مُخَفَّفٌ مُثَقَّـلُ   فَهَـذِهِ أَرْبَعَةٌ تُـفَصَّـلُ

And each of these into the Light or Heavy division,

a total of four, with this subsequent exposition.

- -

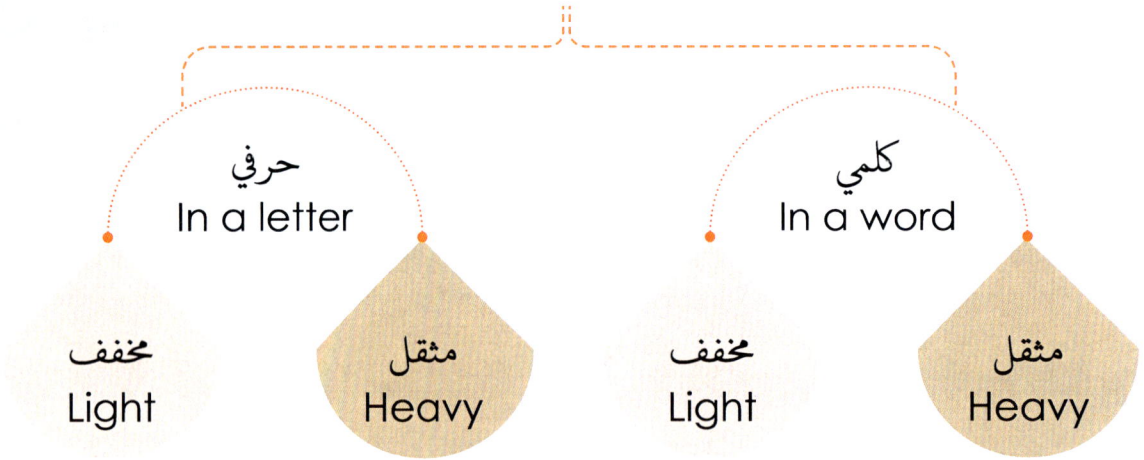

حرفي
In a letter

كلمي
In a word

مخفف
Light

مثقل
Heavy

مخفف
Light

مثقل
Heavy

فَـإِنْ بِكِلْمَـةٍ سُـكُونٌ اجْتَمَـعْ   مَـعْ حَـرْفِ مَـدٍّ فَهْـوَ كِلْمِـيٌّ وَقَـعْ

And if a word embraces sukoon in combination,
  with a madd, it carries the Kalimi designation.

كلمي
In a word

مخفف
Light

مثقل
Heavy

﴿ءَآلۡـَٔنَ وَقَدۡ كُنتُمۡ﴾

﴿ءَآلۡـَٔنَ وَقَدۡ عَصَيۡتَ﴾

﴿حَآجَّكَ﴾   ﴿ضَآلًّا﴾

﴿لَرَآدُّكَ﴾   ﴿دَآبَّةٍ﴾

﴿خَآصَّةً﴾   ﴿كَآفَّةً﴾

﴿بِضَآرِّهِمۡ﴾   ﴿تَحَآضُّونَ﴾

﴿جَآنٌّ﴾   ﴿ءَآمِّينَ﴾

﴿ٱلظَّآنِّينَ﴾   ﴿ضَآلِّينَ﴾

﴿ءَآللَّهُ﴾

أَوْ فِي ثُلاَثِيِّ الحُرُوفِ وُجِدَا   وَالمَدُّ وَسْطُهُ فَحَرْفِيٌّ بَدَا

And if in three disjointed letters both arise,
with madd at the center, then the Harfi term applies.

كِلاَهُمَا مُثَقَّلٌ إِنْ أُدْغِمَا   مُخَفَّفٌ كُلٌّ إِذَا لَمْ يُدْغَمَا

Both of these3 are muthaqqal in the case of idgham,
and conversely mukhaffaf when there is no idgham.

وَاللاَّزِمُ الْحَرفِيُّ أَوَّلَ السُّوَرْ   وُجُودُهُ وَفِي ثَمَانٍ انْحَصَرْ

The Lazim Harfi Madd in the start of the chapters
is found, and encompassed in eight distinct letters,

﴿الٓمٓر﴾	﴿الٓر﴾	﴿الٓمٓصٓ﴾	﴿الٓمٓ﴾
﴿طسٓ﴾	﴿طسٓمٓ﴾	﴿طه﴾	﴿كٓهيعٓصٓ﴾
﴿حمٓ ① عٓسٓقٓ﴾	﴿حمٓ﴾	﴿صٓ﴾	﴿يسٓ﴾
	﴿نٓ﴾	﴿قٓ﴾	

These 8 letters can be 6 beats long

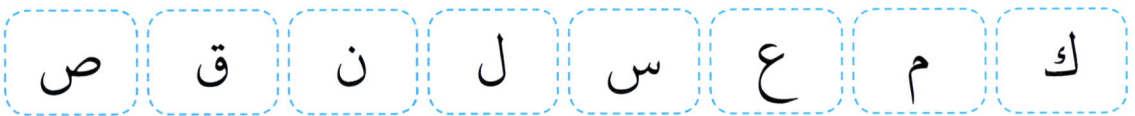

ص	ق	ن	ل	س	ع	م	ك

يَجْمَعُهَا حُرُوفُ كَمْ عَسَلْ نَقَصْ   وَعَيْنُ ذُو وَجْهَيْنِ وَالطُّولُ أَخَصْ

Contained within the Kam ‘Asal Naqas expression;
and while ‘ayn has two ways,6 preferred is prolongation.

The best is make Ayn 6 beats long   ﴿كٓهيعٓصٓ﴾

The Ayn is prolonged for 4 or 6 beats long   ﴿عٓسٓقٓ﴾

وَمَا سِوَي الحَرْفِ الثُّلاَثِيْ لاَ أَلِــفْ   فَمُــدُّهُ مَــدّاً طَبِيعِــيّاً أُلِــفْ

And those apart from the trilateral, alif excluding,

     for their madd, the natural type is more deserving.

Table of letters

Letters	Length of madd
س، ن، ق، ص، ل، ك، م	6 beats madd laazim
ع	4 or 6 beats
ح، ي، ط، ه، ر	2 beats maddul-aslee
ا (الألف)	0 - no madd

وَذَاكَ أَيْضـاً فِي فَـوَاتِحِ السُّـوَرْ   فِي لَفْظِ حَيٍّ طَاهِرٍ قَـدِ انْحَصَــرْ

And these are also found in the openings of the chapters,

     and in the expression Hayyun Tahirun captured.

وَيَجْمَــعُ الْفَوَاتِــحَ الأَرْبَــعْ عَشَــرْ   صِلْـهُ سُـحَيْراً مَـنْ قَطَعْـك ذَا اشْـتَهَرْ

And the fourteen of the chapter openings are arrayed,

     in what they say: Restore the bonds without delay,

     of the kin that cut the way.

﴿المر﴾	﴿الر﴾	﴿المص﴾	﴿الم﴾
﴿طس﴾	﴿طسم﴾	﴿طه﴾	﴿كهيعص﴾
﴿حم ۱ عسق﴾	﴿حم﴾	﴿ص﴾	﴿يس﴾
	﴿ن﴾	﴿ق﴾	

Length of Fir'i Mudood

Due to Sukoon

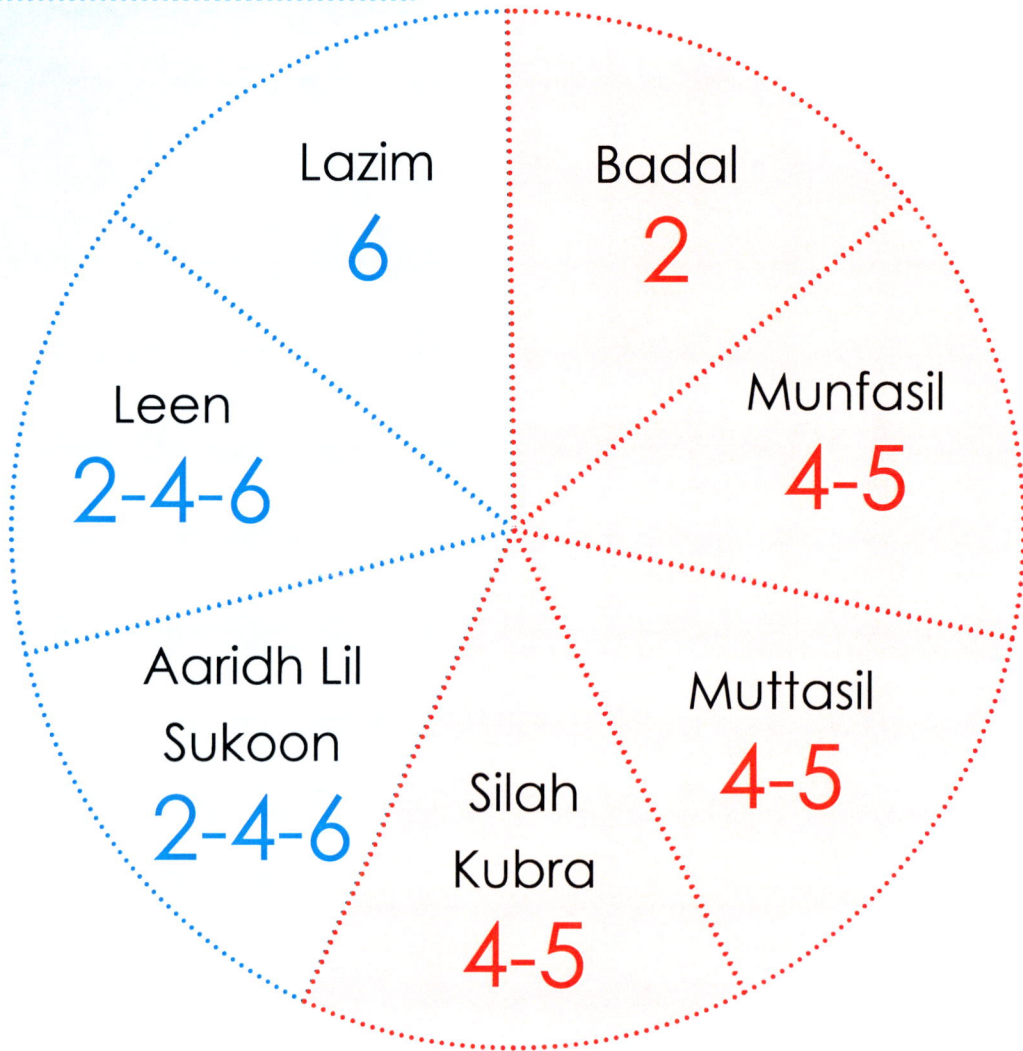

Lazim
6

Badal
2

Munfasil
4-5

Leen
2-4-6

Muttasil
4-5

Aaridh Lil Sukoon
2-4-6

Silah Kubra
4-5

Due to Hamzah

Chapter one

Conclusion
الخاتمة

وَتَــمَّ ذَا النَّــظْمُ بِحَــمْدِ اللَّــهِ   عَلَــى تَمَامِــهِ بِــلاَ تَــنَاهِى

This ode comes now to its conclusion,
    with profuse thanks to Allah for its completion.

أَبْيَاتُــهُ نَــدٌّ بَــدَا لِــذِى النُّــهَى   تَارِيخُــهُ بُشْــرَى لِمَــنْ يُتْقِنُــهَا

Its verses are fragrant for those who possess ingenuity,
    and its date ..... salutation for those who commit it to memory.

ثُــمَّ الصَّــلاَةُ وَالسَّــلاَمُ أَبَــداً   عِلــى خِــتَامِ الأَنْبِــيَاءِ أَحْمَــدَا

And eternal may His salutations be,
    upon Ahmad, the Seal of the Prophecy.

وَالآلِ وَالصَّــحْبِ وَكُــلِّ تَابِــع   وَكُــلِّ قَــارِئٍ وَكُلِّ سَــامِــع

As well as on his noble family and Companions,
    and every follower, recitor and those who listen.

Listen to Tuhfatul Adfaal poem

Scan QR

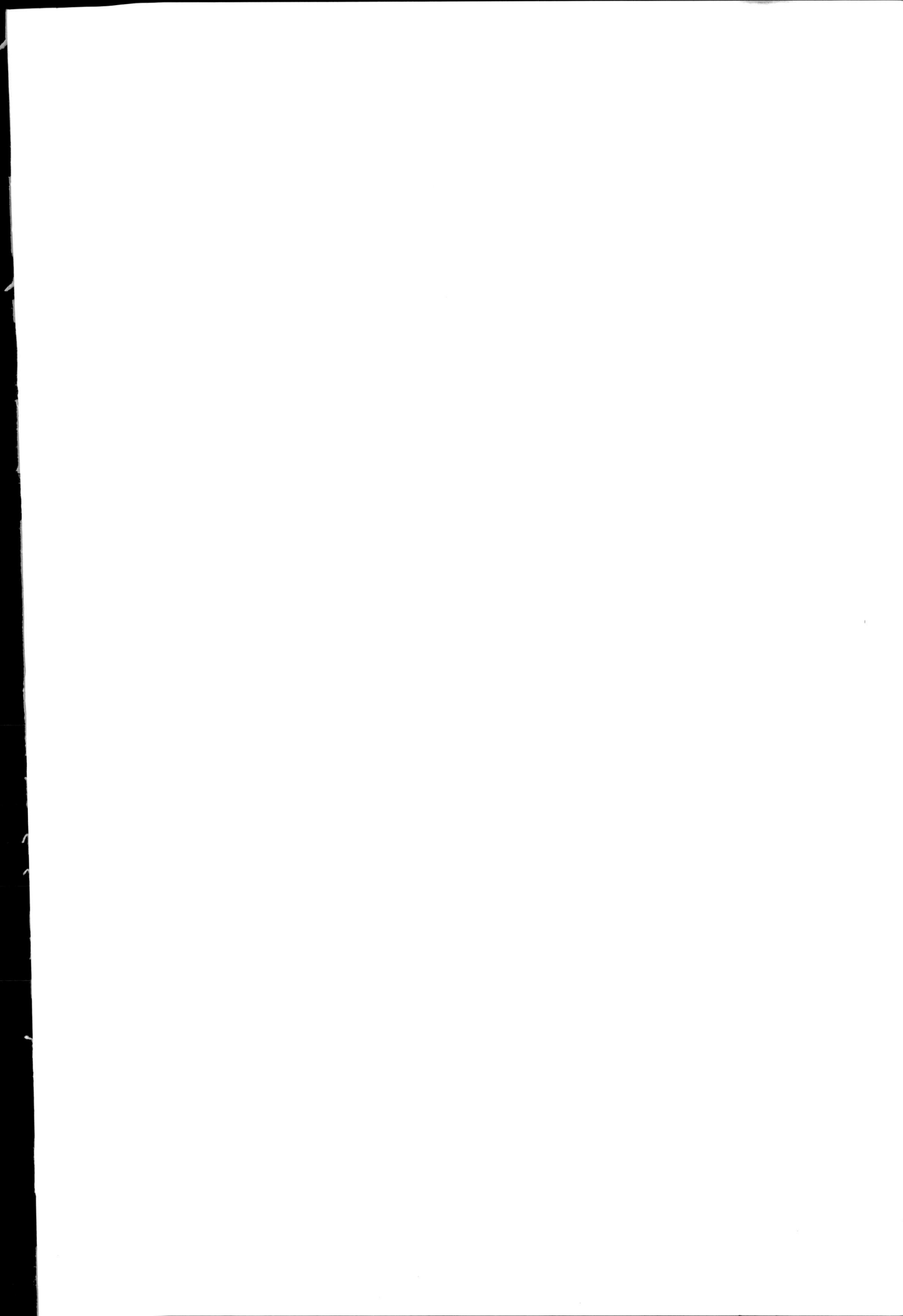

Made in United States
North Haven, CT
06 December 2024